MANCHESTER
CITY COUNCIL

...ide

...ͳe

D1313472

Please return/renew this item
by the last date shown.
Books may also be renewed by
phone or the internet.

Tel: 0161 254 7777

www.manchester.gov.uk/libraries

The bronze revolution

When early humans wanted an axe, knife or arrowhead, they used stone to make it. But stone is heavy, and hard to shape. So eventually, people began to work with metal instead.

Metals like copper and gold were used at first, but they are quite soft and bendy. They made great small tools and jewellery, but weren't so good for weapons.

Then, around 6,000 years ago, people found that when copper was mixed with other metals, it became much stronger. They'd discovered bronze.

a British bronze axe from around 1400 BCE

a 350,000-year-old stone axe from Spain

A new world

In many parts of the world, bronze changed everything. It made brilliant weapons, tools, **ploughs**, armour and all kinds of other ancient objects, from toys and tweezers to money and musical instruments.

This book will take you back in time, to explore and experience some amazing Bronze-Age objects, and the cultures that created them.

What is culture?

Culture means the ways people behave and the things they invent, create or believe. "A culture" can also mean a human group or society who have their own culture.

a Bronze-Age bull figure from Turkey, dated around 2200 BCE

3

What is bronze?

Bronze is a mixture of copper – the main ingredient – and another metal. It's normally made of copper and tin, but it can contain other minerals, like aluminium, zinc or arsenic.

Early people collected metals from rocks by heating them, so the metal melted and flowed out. The first bronze was probably made by accident, as different metals flowed from the rocks and mixed together.

copper

tin

bronze

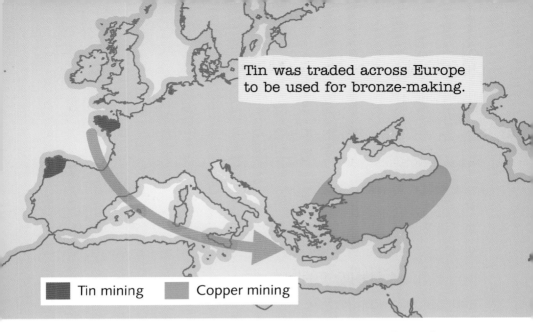

Tin was traded across Europe to be used for bronze-making.

Tin mining Copper mining

Later, people deliberately collected different metals and mixed them to make bronze. Copper and tin usually came from different places, so they had to be transported over long distances.

Why was bronze so useful? It wasn't only harder and stronger than copper, but easier to melt, mould and shape.

Bronze weapons were better on the battlefield. An army with strong, sharp bronze weapons was more powerful against an enemy using weapons made of copper.

Bronze tools also made everyday tasks easier, giving people more time to develop other aspects of life, such as writing and inventing.

Around the world

The Bronze Age happened in many different parts of the world, though not all at the same time. Like many discoveries, it started in the area that's now Iraq, Syria and Iran, often known as Mesopotamia.

From there, bronze-making knowledge spread east across Asia, and west across Europe and into Africa. Far away across the Atlantic, people in the Americas also developed their own bronze, before explorers from Europe went there.

In this book, you'll explore the Bronze-Age world, visiting all the places shown on this map.

North America

20 South America

Culture file: Mesopotamia

Mesopotamia was one of the most important places in the ancient world. It contains two great rivers, the Tigris and the Euphrates, and is a green, **fertile**, warm area where early people could survive easily. The invention of the wheel, and early developments in farming, writing and mathematics, are all thought to have happened here. During the Bronze Age, cultures in Mesopotamia included the Sumerians, Babylonians and Assyrians.

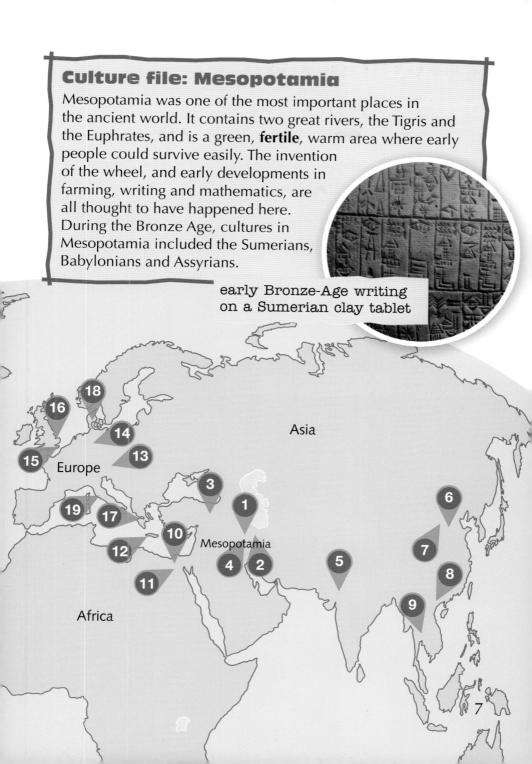

early Bronze-Age writing on a Sumerian clay tablet

Asia

Europe

Mesopotamia

Africa

Farming with bronze

You've landed on the first stop on your tour. You're in Mesopotamia, in 3000 BCE – and it's time to get to work. You'll need a pickaxe like this to help in the crop fields. Ancient Mesopotamia has large cities, with thousands of people who need food.

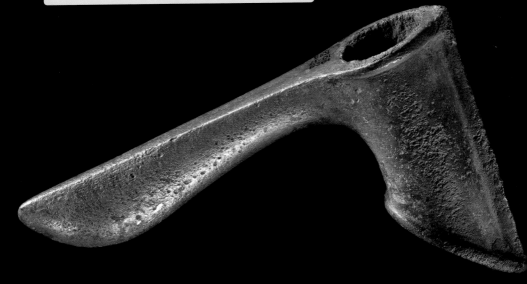

1 Mesopotamian pickaxe head
Found: western Iran
Date: 3000–2000 BCE

Get digging!

Your axe head is attached to a wooden handle. It can be used for breaking up hard ground, digging up weeds, or harvesting the crop once it's grown. The crops could be things like wheat, barley, onions, or sesame plants, grown for their seeds and oil.

sesame plants

Multi-purpose

Axes like this can also be used as weapons, and for other jobs like breaking up wood or digging useful rocks out of the ground.

Did you know?

Farming is thought to have begun in this area around 10,000 years before modern times. Before that, humans hunted wild animals and gathered wild plants. Farming allows people to keep crops and animals in one place, for a steady food supply.

Inventing the wheel

When you arrive in ancient Sumeria, you might be surprised to find little models like this one. But they represent one of the greatest inventions of all time – the wheel.

The wheel first appeared in Mesopotamia in around 3500 BCE, though it may have been invented in other places and at other times as well. By 1000 BCE, it's a normal part of life, used on war chariots and farm carts.

2 Sumerian bronze model chariot
Found: western Iran Date: around 1000 BCE
Some of the models have four wheels, and some have two, like a racing chariot.

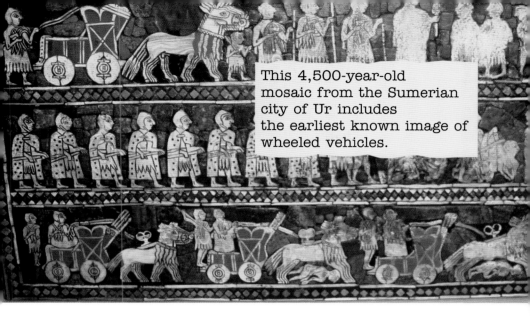

This 4,500-year-old mosaic from the Sumerian city of Ur includes the earliest known image of wheeled vehicles.

What are they for?

In the 21st century, no one is sure whether the models are meant to be **ornaments**, accurate models, or children's toys. What do you think?

Culture file: throwing pots

Sumerians also use wheels another way – for making beautiful pots and vases. The potter's wheel is a single, flat wheel that spins around as you shape a clay pot on top.

Into battle!

Watch out – you've just landed in the middle of a war zone! It's 800 BCE and you're in the ancient region of Urartu in modern-day Turkey, Iran and Armenia. And, as usual, the Urartians are battling their neighbours, the Assyrians.

3 Urartu helmet
Found: eastern Turkey
Date: 900–800 BCE
Urartian helmets have a distinctive pointy shape.

Warmongers

The Urartians are always fighting other groups and trying to take them over – and during 900–800 BCE, they often succeed. So grab this Urartian bronze helmet, and you'll be on the winning side!

Whose helmet is this?

If the helmet is plain, it'll probably be worn by a **rank-and-file** soldier. As it's decorated with detailed patterns and images, it's more likely to belong to an army leader, nobleman or king.

Culture file: Urartian culture

The Urartian people spoke a language that's now **extinct**, but experts have **decoded** their writings to find out about their wars, gods and kings. They were great bronze workers, making weapons and armour, bowls, belt buckles, bells and animal figures.

Riding gear

It's 700 BCE in the Luristan area of Iran, and you're on horseback! Your horse has a bridle and reins, and a bronze bit with two ornate "cheekpieces" on the sides.

Having your own horse, with valuable bronze **tack** made by skilled craftworkers, is the sign of a wealthy noble or royal. Rich people can even have their horses buried with them when they die.

4 Bronze bit and cheekpieces
Found: western Iran
Date: 800–700 BCE
Luristan cheekpieces are often shaped like fantastical animals.

14

Story of the horse

Coinciding with the start of the Bronze Age, around 3500 BCE, people began to tame and breed wild horses. This first happened in central Asia, and spread across the rest of Asia and Europe. By the time of the Luristan culture, horses play a vital part in transport, farming and warfare.

how the cheekpieces are used

Culture file: Luristan bronzes

Many beautiful bronze objects have been found in Luristan: riding gear, pins, rings, brooches, ornaments and cups. We know very little about the culture that made them. But as the items are mostly small and lightweight, they probably belong to **nomadic** people who move around a lot.

Toy animals

Your next stop is the Indus Valley civilisation, in 2000 BCE. That's over 4,000 years before the modern age, but you might see a few things here that are familiar from home.

5 Toy animal figure
Found: India
Date: around 2000 BCE
Wheeled toys like this can be pulled along on a string.

The Indus Valley people, or Harappans, construct neatly planned cities using perfectly shaped bricks, and have drainage systems, swimming pools, and the first flushing toilets!

Indus Valley bronze

The Harappans bring the same attention to detail to their bronze work. They use bronze for making smaller items – spearheads, plates and bowls, clothes pins, bells and bracelets. Most of all, they make little statues, animal figures and toys, like this wheeled bronze rhinoceros.

Culture file: making seals

The Indus Valley people also make seals – small stamps that can be used to press marks into clay. The marks include symbols that look like writing, but right into the 21st century, no one has been able to figure out what they mean.

each seal features an animal and several symbols

Off with his head!

You've travelled far across Asia to the home of the ancient Chinese Shang **dynasty**. No one is as good with bronze as the Shang. Over the centuries of their **reign**, they've perfected a skilful bronze-casting method. It allows them to create all kinds of jars, jugs, cauldrons, musical instruments and weapons, with beautifully detailed designs.

The Shang use several sections joined together to make moulds for casting bronze items. This picture shows how a container called a "ding" is made.

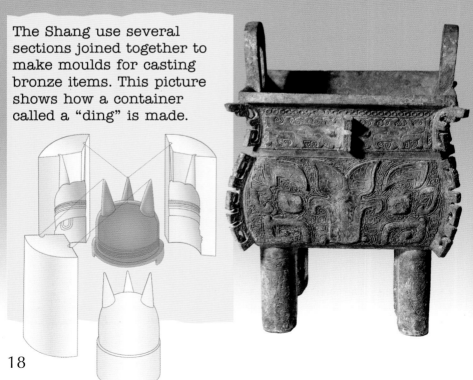

6 **Shang dynasty axe**
Found: China
Date: 1500–1000 BCE
This type of bronze
axe is called a "yue".

Watch out!

Make sure you don't get
captured as a prisoner
of war, or become a rich nobleman's servant.
You could end up being horribly sacrificed and sent
to accompany your king or
leader into the grave. To make
the sacrifice, the executioner
might use a bronze
ceremonial axe with a scary
face, like this one.

Culture file: Shang inventions

Besides making amazing
bronzes, the Shang invented
an early form of writing,
a calendar and chopsticks!

Cowrie coins

Zoom forward in time
a few hundred years, and you're in
the time of the Zhou dynasty, who
overthrew the Shang in 1046 BCE.

Culture file: bronze bells

The bronze-making of the Zhou and other Chinese peoples of
the time shows the influence of the Shang dynasty that came
before them. They make some amazing creations, like this
"bianzhong", a xylophone-like musical instrument made up of
65 bells.

The instrument was found in a tomb
dating from around 433 BCE.

Shell money

In ancient China, cowrie shells, a type of seashell, have been used as money for centuries. Many other civilisations use them too. But the shells have to be collected from the coast, and they aren't always easy to find.

Do it yourself!

Instead, the ancient Chinese have begun to make their own "cowrie shell" money out of other materials – like clay, bone, stone, **jade**, or bronze. Bronze cowries are among the world's first metal coins.

7 Zhou dynasty bronze cowrie coins
Found: China
Date: around 1000 BCE
The holes in the imitation cowries mean you can thread them on to a string to keep them handy.

Picture drum

By 300 BCE, the Bronze Age is over in many places, but in northern Vietnam, it's reached its peak. The Dong Son people are skilled bronze-makers, and cast incredible detail into their work. They're most famous for their ceremonial drums.

Dong Son drum
Found: Vietnam   Date: 300 BCE
The drums range from hand-sized to over a metre tall.

Beat the drum

To play the drum, you need to hang it up from a pole or crossbar by its handles, to allow it to **resonate**. You then beat it with drumsticks. How do we know? The Dong Son drums are covered with pictures, including several showing the drums themselves being played.

modern Vietnamese musicians play a Dong Son drum

The Dong Son people use the drums during battles and at feasts and festivals. They are also a symbol of wealth and power, as each one is expensive and takes a long time to make.

Culture file: Dong Son life

The scenes on the drums also reveal many other details of Dong Son culture. They show people growing rice, fighting, dancing and holding boat races, processions and parties, as well as lots of images of birds and animals.

Jewellery for the afterlife

Next you're off to nearby Thailand, to visit the ancient civilisation of Ban Chiang. The people here have their own style of bronze craft, making axes and spearheads, knives, hooks, vases, ladles and **unique**, chunky jewellery. You could try on a butterfly bracelet, a heavy arm-cuff or a torque – a rigid, ring-shaped necklace.

Culture file: grave goods

Many cultures, from the ancient Egyptians to the ancient Chinese, have buried dead people with piles of treasure, everyday items or money, known as grave goods. This provides the person with everything they need for their journey to the **afterlife**. It can also be a symbol of their importance and wealth.

an excavated Ban Chiang grave

These items often end up in graves, where they're buried along with the dead. The graves also contain the local style of pottery, with its unusual red and white patterns.

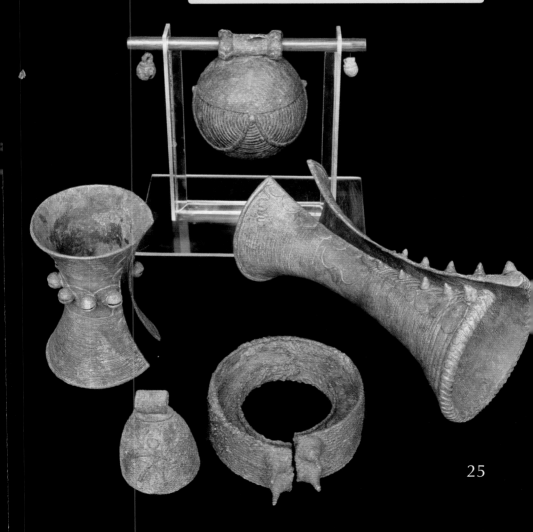

⑨ Ban Chiang jewellery
Found: Thailand
Date: 1000–200 BCE
These objects have a greenish coating, but are made of bronze.

Making a mummy

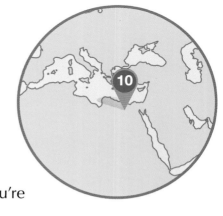

You're leaving Asia, and heading to ancient Egypt in Africa, to see how mummies are made. Hope you're not squeamish!

10

Did you know?

The ancient Egyptians existed long before the Bronze Age, but began using bronze when it was introduced to them from other cultures, in around 3000 BCE.

This Egyptian art shows the embalmer, or mummy-maker, at work wearing a mask of Anubis, the Egyptian god of mummification.

Body bits

The Egyptians are famous for the way they mummify, or preserve, dead people before burying them. To do this, they cut the body open and remove the internal organs, then cover the body with salt and other chemicals to stop it from rotting.

These Egyptian bronze knives and hooks are thought to be tools for doing these rather gruesome jobs.

10 Bronze knives and hooks
Found: Egypt
Date: around 600 BCE
Besides hooks and knives, the mummy-makers use bronze tweezers and needles.

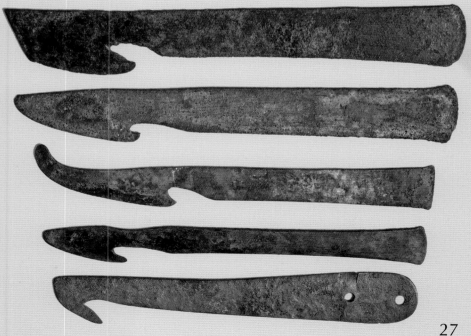

Cat with an earring

When you're in ancient Egypt, you'll notice there are quite a lot of cats around. The Egyptians love their cats! They're seen as a **sacred** animal, and many people have them as pets. Sometimes, when a cat dies, it's mummified just as humans are. Later, when its owner dies, they're buried together.

ancient Egyptian cat mummy

Bronze Bastet

The Egyptians also make beautiful cat statues, often out of bronze. They represent Bastet, who is the goddess of cats, and also of the home, warmth, motherhood and children. These statues often have an earring. Some real cats in ancient Egypt also have their ears pierced, and wear earrings and necklaces!

11 Bronze cat statue
Found: Egypt
Date: around 600 BCE
Beautiful cat statues like this are often kept in temples to honour the goddess Bastet.

Killer weapon

You may have been to the Greek island of Crete before, but in 2000 BCE, it's quite different! Knossos, on Crete, is a huge **complex** of palace buildings and cemeteries. It's the centre of the Minoan civilisation, which dominates Greece at this time.

Travel and trade

The Minoans are a seafaring people and are famous for their trade links to other lands around the Mediterranean Sea. They trade in metals such as gold, and tin for making bronze, as well as ivory, wood, olive oil, wine and wool. Because of this, they are often seen as a peaceful people, but the Minoans can fight when they need to. They use bronze to make their weapons, such as axes, spears, daggers and razor-sharp swords.

12 Minoan bronze sword

Found: Crete, Greece
Date: 2000–1500 BCE

This bronze sword with a golden handle was found in a tomb near Knossos.

This Minoan bronze sculpture shows someone leaping over a bull, probably as part of a religious ritual.

Culture file: Minoan bulls

In the Minoan religion, bulls are seen as sacred, and they often make bronze bull models and sculptures.

Getting dressed

Heading west from Greece, as bronze technology spreads across Europe, you reach Austria. The people who live here are mysterious – not much is known about them. But items found in their graves show they have developed their own style for making delicate bronze jewellery.

You can see where these people's pins were carefully placed in their graves.

Culture file: Special burials

When these people bury their dead, they lay them curled up on their sides, with their pins and other jewellery arranged on or around them in the grave. Men and women are positioned in different directions.

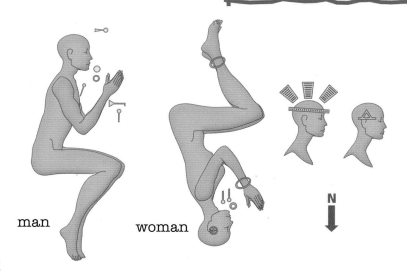

man   woman

N

Everyday objects

Bronze is strong and can be made into sharp objects – but that doesn't just mean weapons. It's also perfect for everyday household tools, like pins and needles. These pins, called wheel pins and disk pins, can be used to fasten the fabric of a cape or robe, so that it doesn't fall off. Or they can be worn as a decoration, like a brooch.

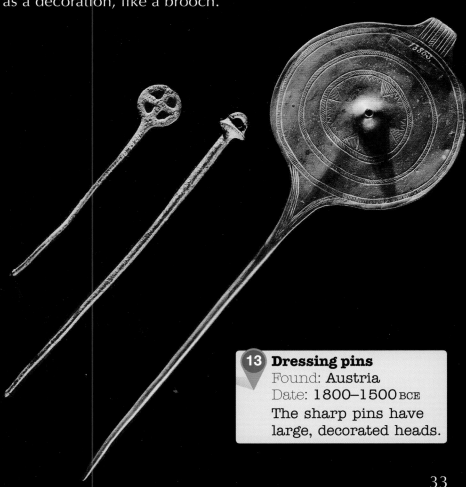

13 Dressing pins
Found: Austria
Date: 1800–1500 BCE
The sharp pins have large, decorated heads.

Mysterious space disc

It's 1600 BCE, and you've landed in what will one day be Germany. At your feet is an extraordinary, blue-green bronze disc, decorated with gold. It's unlike anything else you've seen on your travels.

Looking at the sky

The local people here have a unique culture. They're known as the Unetice people, after a Czech village, but they live across a wide area. And what this strange object reveals is that they're really interested in the sky. The disc seems to show a sun (or maybe a full moon), a new moon, and several constellations.

Sky disc

Two curved bands at the sides of the disc show the range of positions of the rising and setting sun. So this could be some kind of calendar or sky-watching guide. Or it could be for religious ceremonies, or just a beautiful decorative object belonging to a wealthy leader.

14 **Nebra Sky Disc**
Found: Germany   Date: around 1600 BCE
Back in the present day, the disc can be seen in the
State Museum of Prehistory in Halle, Germany.

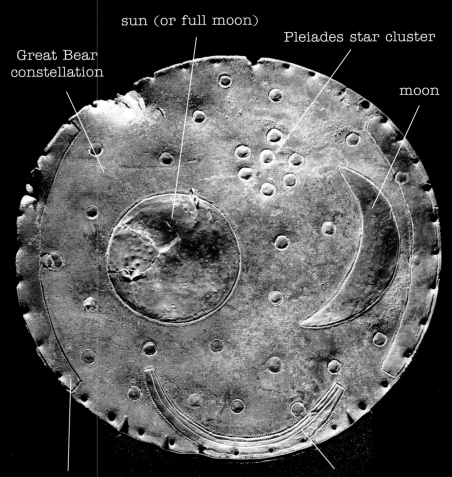

sun (or full moon)

Pleiades star cluster

Great Bear
constellation

moon

horizon bands, showing
where the sun rises
and sets

sun boat (many early peoples
imagine the sun riding in a
boat or chariot)

30 cm

Out to sea

For the next leg of your tour, you're not on land – you're in a boat on the water! You're in the sea, off southern England, home of the Dover Bronze-Age Boat.

Wood, not bronze

Unlike the other objects you've seen, this one isn't made of bronze. Bronze-Age people crisscross the seas in boats, trading in metals, foods and other products. But their boats rarely survive into later times, because they are made of wood, which rots away easily.

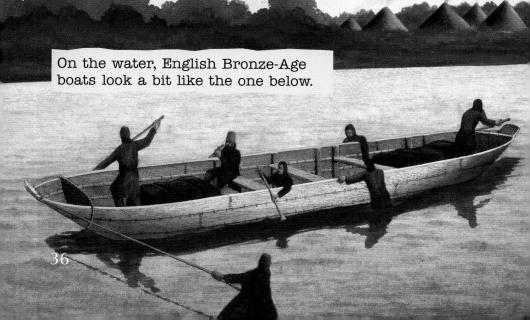

On the water, English Bronze-Age boats look a bit like the one below.

15 Bronze-Age boat
Found: England
Date: around 1550 BCE
Back in the modern age, the remains of the Dover boat can be seen at the Dover Museum in England.

This one, which will lie buried for over 3,000 years before being rediscovered, is an exception. It's a shallow, open vessel, made of planks of wood, held together with flexible yew tree twigs. Found near Dover on England's south coast, it's built for sea journeys, and can probably cross the English Channel.

Bent dagger

Next stop: Norfolk, in eastern
England, 3,500 years before
modern times. In Bronze-Age Britain,
people often carry weapons with them,
to settle disputes and protect themselves
from enemies. A typical one is a bronze dirk –
a small, sharp dagger.

16 Folded dirk
Found: England
Date: around 1500 BCE
You can tell the giant
dirk isn't an everyday
dagger, as it has no parts
for fixing it to a handle.

This is a usable, normal-sized
dirk, with a part that could be
fixed to a handle. It was found
in Cambridgeshire, England.

There's a bronze dirk blade right in front of you – but it's no use at all! It's far too big to carry around, it's blunt and it's been bent in half. What's the point of that?

Religious ritual

For Bronze-Age people, this isn't a pointless dirk, but an extra-precious one, made to be part of a religious ceremony. The giant blade will never be attached to a handle. Instead, it's bent to show that it's not for normal use, and buried as a sacrifice to the gods.

Suit of armour

Where next? You're going to ancient Greece, back to the time of the Mycenaeans. These bold, battle-loving Greeks are around from about 1600–1100 BCE. They feature in the works of the great poet Homer, who tells the story of the legendary war they waged against the city of Troy.

Warrior wear

The Mycenaeans are great bronze-workers and fierce fighters. To join one of their many attacks on neighbouring peoples, you'll need to protect yourself with a suit of bronze armour like this. Known as the Dendra armour, it'll spend many years in one of the Mycenaeans' tombs, where treasures and weapons are buried along with their owners.

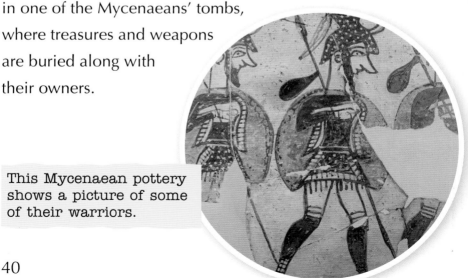

This Mycenaean pottery shows a picture of some of their warriors.

The armour is mostly bronze, but the helmet isn't. It's made of something completely different – sliced-up boar's tusks! Helmets like this are mentioned in Homer's poems.

gorget or collar

shoulder guards

cuirass or chest plate

holes for threading the sections together with leather cords

skirt pieces

17 Dendra armour
Found: Greece
Date: around
1450 BCE
The armour is made of sheets of bronze, formed by hammering the metal into shape.

41

Shaving kit

Head north, and you're in
chilly Scandinavia. It's taken a long
time for bronze technology to
spread here, and it has its own mini
Bronze Age, called the Nordic Bronze Age.
Nordic people must **import** their bronze from
further south, but they have perfected their own crafting style.

Culture file: Nordic culture

Though they don't seem to use writing, the metal objects,
monuments and rock carvings of the Nordic Bronze-Age people
reveal clues about their society. They worship the sun, get food
by farming and hunting, and
are great seafarers.

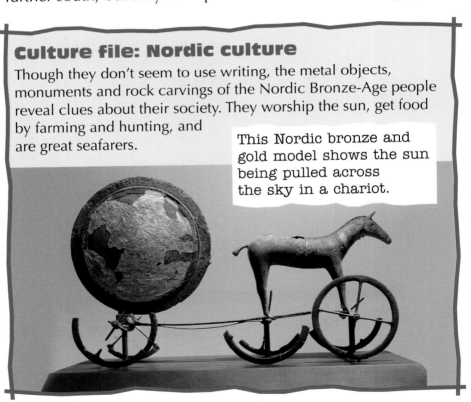

This Nordic bronze and
gold model shows the sun
being pulled across
the sky in a chariot.

Looking good!

In many societies, a man's weapons and armour are buried with him when he dies, especially if he was a great warrior. Here, men's graves also contain vanity kits – bronze razors, tweezers, and tools that could be used for trimming and cleaning fingernails. This suggests that appearance is very important to Nordic Bronze-Age men.

18 Nordic Bronze-Age razors
Found: Denmark
Date: 1100–500 BCE
Razors are often decorated with detailed patterns and pictures.

In the mirror

You've arrived in ancient northern Italy, home of the unique Etruscan civilisation – and you're invited to the feast!

Party time!

The **murals** the Etruscans make inside their tombs reveal that they love a banquet. These are important occasions in Etruscan life, where people show off their wealth, hospitality and status in society.

The murals show partygoers, musicians and dancers often wearing decorations and hairstyles, colourful clothes and jewellery. Perhaps this is why the Etruscans also have a lot of mirrors! Before modern glass mirrors, these are often made from polished stone or metal. The Etruscans make them from bronze, decorated with beautiful images.

19 **Etruscan bronze mirror**
Found: Italy
Date: 500–400 BCE
This mirror has an image of a lion on it.

Culture file: Greek chic

Though the Etruscans have their own culture, they are big fans of the Greeks too. They often use scenes from Greek legends, and copy Greek art styles.

Brain surgery

To experience bronze-making in the Americas, you have to travel forward in time to around 600 CE. You're in Peru, in the time of the Moche people. And let's hope you don't have a headache! The Moche have a treatment for that, and it's not much fun.

The Moche are known for their distinctive pottery, such as animal-shaped bottles.

Bone cutter

This strangely shaped bronze knife isn't a kitchen tool – it's a **surgical** instrument. The Moche use it for trepanning, or cutting holes in people's skulls. This is done as a medical treatment, probably to try to cure headaches or other illnesses. Amazingly, skulls have been found with holes that had started to heal, showing the patient survived!

Did you know?

The Moche weren't the only people to try trepanning – trepanned skulls have been found in many other parts of the world too.

20 Bronze surgical knife

Found: **Peru**
Date: **100–800** CE

The knife is gripped by the handle at the top, and used to make several straight cuts in the skull to remove a square section of bone.

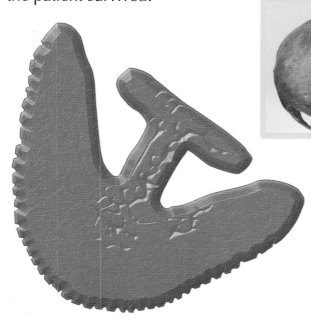

The end of the Bronze Age

The Bronze Age ended at different times in
different places. The first major changes happened in
the eastern Mediterranean and Mesopotamia, where
the Bronze Age had first begun.

The great Bronze-Age collapse

Many of the great civilisations in this area collapsed or came
to an end around 1200–1100 BCE. This may have been because
of wars, volcanic eruptions, or climate problems such
as drought.

A huge volcanic eruption on the island
of Thera, north of Crete, around
1500 BCE, may have caused long-term
problems for cultures in the area.

Europe

Turkey

Greece

Mesopotamia

Thera eruption

Crete

Egypt

Some experts think bronze itself could have played a part. Bronze weapons were so strong and effective, they may have led to deadlier wars, with people finding it easier to overthrow their leaders or other kingdoms.

Here comes the Iron Age!

In other areas, the Bronze Age carried on for hundreds more years. Eventually, though, a new age, the Iron Age, took over. Iron is harder to **extract** and work with than bronze. But once people learnt to use it, it became the metal of choice, as it was cheaper and easier to find.

a helmet and sword with scabbard from the early Iron Age

Bronze and the modern world

The Bronze Age is ancient history, but bronze itself isn't. During the Iron Age, it continued to be an important metal, and it's still used today.

Piano and bass guitar strings are often partly made of bronze, and so are percussion instruments like bells and cymbals. We award bronze medals for third place in a sports contest. Artists still often choose beautiful, warm-coloured bronze for sculptures.

the famous 19th century bronze sculpture "The Thinker", by French sculptor Auguste Rodin

the steel-covered Walt Disney Concert Hall in Los Angeles, USA, built in 2003

However, in today's world, iron remains the more important metal. It's especially widespread in the form of super-strong, durable steel, which is iron mixed with carbon or other chemicals.

Long-lasting bronze

Thanks to bronze's toughness and long-lasting qualities, thousands of amazing objects from the Bronze Age have survived. Many of them are perfectly preserved, and on display in museums. Others are probably still in the ground, waiting for someone to find them. What might we dig up next?

Glossary

afterlife   the life that exists after death, according to some cultures and religions

BCE   Before the Common Era (previously known as BC)

CE   Common Era (previously known as AD)

complex   an arrangement of buildings that are used as a group

decoded   made sense of, understood or translated

dynasty   a long line of rulers from the same family

extinct   no longer living or in use

extract   remove something from the place it's found in, such as the ground

fertile   with rich soil that's good for growing crops in

import   bring something into a country from another country or land

jade   a very hard, greenish stone often used for making ornaments or small objects

murals   wall paintings

nomadic   moving from place to place, with no fixed home

ornaments   objects made as decorations, usually with no practical use

plough   farming tool with a blade that's pulled through the soil to turn it over

rank-and-file   ordinary members of a group, or soldiers in an army

reign   the period of time that a monarch or dynasty rules over their kingdom

resonate   produce a loud sound for a long time

sacred   connected to a god or gods, or having an important role in a religion

surgical   to do with medical operations on the body

tack   equipment used for riding a horse, such as saddles, bridles and stirrups

unique   one of a kind, and unlike anything else

Index

Around the Bronze-Age world

Americas

Moche bronze
surgical knife

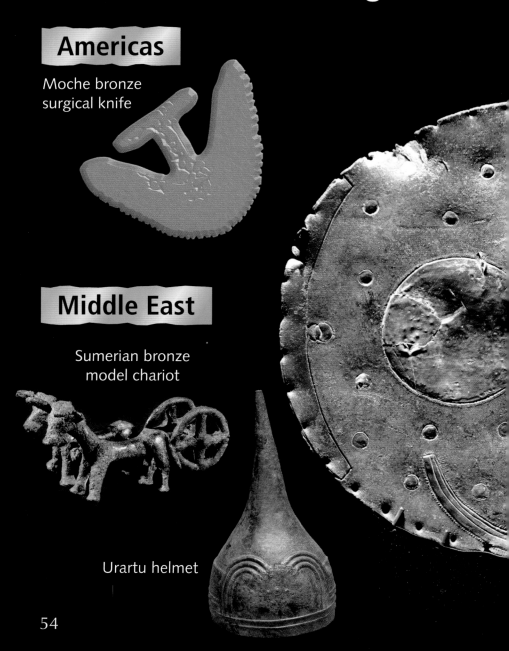

Middle East

Sumerian bronze
model chariot

Urartu helmet

Europe

Minoan bronze
sword

Nebra Sky Disc

Etruscan
bronze mirror

Asia

Indus Valley
toy animal
figure

Ban Chiang
jewellery

Africa

Egyptian cat
with an earring

55

Ideas for reading

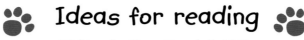

Written by Clare Dowdall, PhD
Lecturer and Primary Literacy Consultant

Reading objectives:
- draw inferences and justify these with evidence
- predict what might happen from details stated and implied
- retrieve, record and present information from non-fiction

Spoken language objectives:
- give well-structured descriptions, explanations and narratives for different purposes
- participate in discussions, presentations, performances, role play, improvisations and debates

Curriculum links: History – changes in Britain from the Stone Age to the Iron Age. Geography – locational knowledge

Resources: ICT; paper and pens.

Build a context for reading

- Look at the front cover and read the title. Ask children to suggest what they think the image is showing.
- Read the blurb together. Create a simple time line to locate the Bronze Age with any other known historical eras, e.g. the Romans, the Egyptians. Check that children know the terms Before the Common Era (BCE) and Common Era (CE).
- Discuss what bronze is and what's special about it (it's a metal, long-lasting, has left evidence, can be made into objects).

Understand and apply reading strategies

- Turn to the contents. Ask children to skim read through, looking for items that intrigue them.
- Ask children to read pp2–5 in pairs. Develop their understanding by asking them to make a spider diagram as they read to collect key facts.
- Discuss the key facts collected, and their impression of the Bronze Age based on this introduction.